BUSINESS INNOVATIONS MADE BY MISTAKE

ORIGINAL MAUVEINE PREPARED BY SIR WILLIAM PERKIN IN 1856

FANTASTIC FAILURES
From Flops to Fortune

MARTIN GITLIN

45TH PARALLEL PRESS

Published in the United States of America by Cherry Lake Publishing Group
Ann Arbor, Michigan
www.cherrylakepublishing.com

Reading Adviser: Beth Walker Gambro, MS, Ed., Reading Consultant, Yorkville, IL
Series Adviser: Virginia Loh-Hagan
Book Designer: Frame25 Productions

Photo Credits: © Science Museum / Science & Society Picture Library, cover, title page; © paulaphoto/Shutterstock, 4; © bbernard/Shutterstock, 5; © fizkes/Shutterstock, 7; © Minnesota Historical Society, 8; © marketlan/Shutterstock, 9; © Ken Wolter/ Shutterstock, 10; © Paosun Rt/Shutterstock, 11; Signe Dons, Public domain, via Wikimedia Commons, 12; Harris & Ewing, photographer, Public domain, via Wikimedia Commons, 15; © fotoknips/Shutterstock, 16; © KOBRIN PHOTO/Shutterstock, 17; © karen roach/Shutterstock, 19; Science History Institute, CC BY-SA 3.0 via Wikimedia Commons, 20; © Sealed Air Corp., 23; © Olivia Rich/Shutterstock, 24; © Isah Kambali/Shutterstock, 25; © Twin Design/Shutterstock, 26; © Hadrian/Shutterstock, 27; © RealPeopleStudio/Shutterstock, 28; © Surasak_Photo/Shutterstock, 29; © Komsan Loonprom/Shutterstock, 32

45th Parallel Press is an imprint of Cherry Lake Publishing Group.

Library of Congress Cataloging-in-Publication Data has been filed and is available at catalog.loc.gov

Library of Congress Cataloging-in-Publication Data

Names: Gitlin, Marty, author.
Title: Business innovations made by mistake / written by Martin Gitlin.
Description: Ann Arbor, Michigan : 45th Parallel Press, [2024] | Series:
  Fantastic failures: from flops to fortune | Audience: Grades 4-6 |
  Summary: "From sticky notes to synthetic dyes, this title highlights
  products that were supposed to be something else entirely. Fantastic
  Failures: From Flops to Fortune takes readers through the unexpected
  origins of popular products and innovations. With a focus on persistence
  and creative thinking, this hi-lo series makes the case that failure
  might just be the first step to success"-- Provided by publisher.
Identifiers: LCCN 2023043469 | ISBN 9781668938225 (hardcover) | ISBN
  9781668939260 (paperback) | ISBN 9781668940600 (ebook) | ISBN
  9781668941959 (pdf)
Subjects: LCSH: Creative ability in business--Juvenile literature. |
  Success in business--Juvenile literature.
Classification: LCC HD53 .G58 2024 | DDC 650.1--dc23/eng/20231026
LC record available at https://lccn.loc.gov/2023043469

Cherry Lake Publishing would like to acknowledge the work of the Partnership for 21st Century Learning, a network of Battelle for Kids. Please visit Battelle for Kids online for more information.

Printed in the United States of America

Note from publisher: Websites change regularly, and their future contents are outside of our control. Supervise children when conducting any recommended online searches for extended learning opportunities.

Contents

INTRODUCTION

"If at first you don't succeed, try, try again." This is an old saying. It's been said a lot. It's a great tip. Failure is part of life. It's not bad. It can have good results. People must not let failure defeat them. They should keep trying. Failing can lead to success.

People in business learn from their mistakes. They know about failing. They have ideas. They invent things. They sell them. They make money. But not all ideas work. Some ideas **flop**. *Flop* means to fail.

Ideas may not work as planned. Successful people don't give up. They solve problems. They find other uses for flops. They turn flops into fortunes.

The business world has many examples. Many great products started as failures. These failures worked out. They made life easier. They helped people at work. They helped people at home.

Successful inventors show **persistence**. Persisting means not quitting. Their hard work paid off. That is a lesson everyone can learn.

CHAPTER 1

Post-it® Notes and Failed Airplane Glue

Almost everyone has seen them. They might not know what to call them. But they've seen them at home. They've seen them in school. They've seen them at work.

They're sticky notes. They're also called Post-it® Notes. They once were only yellow. Now they come in many colors. And they stick to nearly anything.

People use them to write messages. They write to themselves. They write to others. These sticky notes can be easily removed. Or they can stay stuck. They're great reminders. They signal people to do something.

Sticky notes are super useful. They make life easier. Spencer Silver invented them in 1968. He was a scientist. He worked for the 3M company. The 3M company makes office supplies.

Silver was working in his lab. He wanted to invent a new **adhesive**. Adhesives make things stick. Silver used **acrylic**. Acrylic is a sticky material. It's stiff and strong.

Silver invented a glue. His new invention wasn't meant for public use. It was for airplanes. It failed as airplane glue. It didn't stick well enough. Planes need a much stronger bond.

Silver never gave up. He knew his glue was special. He struggled to find a use for it. He told his co-workers. One of them was Art Fry. Fry also worked for 3M.

Art Fry (b. 1931)

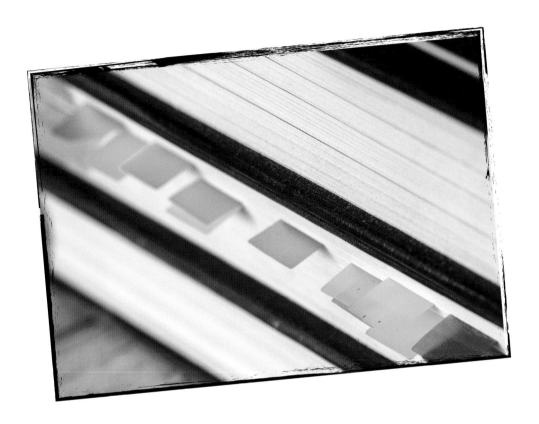

He researched new ideas. Fry often used scraps of paper. He'd mark hymnbooks for church services. But these scraps kept falling out. Fry needed a bookmark that would stick. He also didn't want to damage the pages.

He used Silver's glue. He coated paper with the sticky stuff. He wrote notes on it. He placed them in his hymnbook. The notes stuck. It worked! Post-it® Notes were born.

But the notes weren't ready for sale. There were problems. 3M kept working on it. It tried to perfect it. The glue needed to be stickier. It had to always stay in place.

The product was ready in 1980. It was tested in Boise, Idaho. People loved it. They said they'd buy it. Post-it® Notes went to market. They were a hit.

3M created different Post-it® Notes products. They expanded. They were sold in more than 100 countries. About 50 billion sticky notes are sold each year.

Silver and Fry persisted. They kept working. They improved sticky notes. They worked for many years. They won many awards. Their invention is used every day. It's hard to think about life without sticky notes.

FLOPPED!
Bic's Pen "For Her"

A pen for women? Why would women need their own pen? Nobody really knows. The "For Her" pen failed. This pen was made by Bic. It's the most famous pen company in the United States. It made a foolish mistake in 2012. It created a pen for women. This was a disaster. The pen was pink. It was also purple. People laughed at the idea. Comedians made jokes about it. Women ignored it. Many thought it was sexist. Bic took the pen off the market. The pen was put into the Museum of Failure.

CHAPTER 2

Failed Medicine Makes Synthetic Dye

William Henry Perkin was a great scientist. He started young. He was 18 years old in 1856. He went to the Royal College of Chemistry. The school was in London, England.

Perkin was on vacation. He worked instead of played. He set out to make **synthetic quinine**. Synthetic means produced using chemicals. Quinine is made from tree bark. It helps treat **malaria**. Malaria is a sickness. It's caused by infected mosquito bites. It can kill people.

Perkin wanted to make quinine in a lab. This would make quinine easier to get.

Perkin failed to make quinine. Instead, his **beakers** were filled with sludge. The sludge was dirty. It was brown. Perkin cleaned his beakers. He used alcohol. Then he saw something amazing. The sludge changed color. It turned bright purple. It turns out Perkin invented a **dye**. Dyes add color to something.

William Henry Perkin (1838-1907)

Perkin's mistake was a success. He didn't invent medicine. Instead, he invented synthetic dyes. Before Perkin, dyes were natural. They were taken from plants or metals. This process was costly. It also took much effort. The natural dyes faded fast.

Perkin invented the dyes by accident. His invention made a huge impact. Synthetic dyes are used in many ways. They add color to products. They color clothes. They color paper. They color leather. They color hair. They color much more. Synthetic dyes are more useful than natural dyes. They don't fade when washed. They don't fade when under strong heat or light. The colors stay strong.

Perkin needed to promote his invention. He was young. But he had business sense. He **patented** his dye. Patents are legal rights. They protect people's ideas. Perkin called his dye "mauveine." **Mauve** is a shade of purple.

Perkin's dye was a big success. Queen Victoria ruled England at that time. Her clothes were dyed with mauveine. This made it popular.

Perkin invented more dyes. He made green dyes. He made red dyes. He made violet dyes. He made the world a more colorful place. He made it brighter. There are many good uses for dyes. But there are also bad uses. Some companies dye foods. This makes foods look tastier. Food dyes are used to promote unhealthy food. An example is breakfast cereals. Some are fun colors. But they usually have lots of sugar.

Perkin studied more science. He did other things. But he'd always be known for inventing synthetic dyes. He died in 1907. His work lives on. Colored products are everywhere. There's a medal named after him. It's called the Perkin Medal. It's awarded to a chemist. It's given every year.

FLOPPED!
Harley-Davidson Perfume

Harley-Davidson is a company. It makes motorcycles. It's the most famous motorcycle brand. In 1994, it made a big mistake. It made a **perfume**. Perfumes are liquids with nice smells. They're splashed on human bodies. They make people smell good. The Harley-Davidson perfume flopped. The scent was not good. It was meant to give wearers a special feeling. It was meant to remind people of riding a motorcycle. Its goal was to smell like an open road. But people didn't want to smell like that. Some tried it. But few bought it. Many thought it smelled nasty. Harley-Davidson took it off the market.

CHAPTER 3

400 Failed First Uses for Bubble Wrap

Bubble Wrap is fun. People put the bubbles between their fingers. They press down. They make popping sounds. In this way, Bubble Wrap is a toy. But that is not its intended use. Bubble Wrap is for shipping. It protects items. It keeps them from being broken or damaged. It keeps things safe. It often lines envelopes. It's also placed in boxes.

Two men invented Bubble Wrap. They were Alfred Fielding and Marc Chavannes. It started in 1957.

Fielding and Chavannes were working on another idea. They wanted to make a new kind of wallpaper. They grabbed two pieces of a plastic shower curtain. They put them through a heat-sealing machine. This made a sheet with air bubbles.

Alfred Fielding (1917-1994)

Fielding and Chavannes failed at making wallpaper. But they didn't give up. They did what the best inventors do. They studied other uses for it. They came up with more than 400 ideas. One idea was **greenhouse insulation**. A greenhouse is a building. It's used to grow plants. Insulation is a wall layer. It's used to keep heat in or out.

Fielding and Chavannes tested their product. The bubble sheet didn't work as greenhouse insulation. The scientists kept trying. They called their product Bubble Wrap. They founded the Sealed Air company. But they still had no use for their creation. They just knew it was useful.

Then they had an amazing thought. IBM is a computer company. IBM was making early computer models. Fielding and Chavannes thought of IBM. They knew computers needed to be kept safe. Computers could be damaged during shipping. IBM was using crumpled newspapers. This wasn't good enough. Bubble Wrap was perfect for IBM.

Fielding and Chavannes finally found a use for their product. Bubble Wrap sold like crazy. Companies found it ideal for shipping **fragile** things. Fragile means easily broken.

Fielding and Chavannes kept moving forward. They made different types of Bubble Wrap. Bubble Wrap comes in different shapes. It comes in different sizes. It can be made thicker for extra strength. It can be made in small sheets. It can be made in large sheets. It also had a bonus perk. People loved popping it. Some think this popping relieves stress.

Fielding and Chavannes didn't make a lot of money. They were scientists. They weren't businessmen. Neither wanted to run the company. So they turned it over to T. J. Dermot Dunphy. Dunphy knew business. He added more uses for Bubble Wrap. An example is swimming pool covers. These covers were huge sheets. They trapped sun rays. They retained heat. This kept the pool water warm.

Dunphy made Bubble Wrap popular. Sales soared. Today, Bubble Wrap is big business. It makes more than $5 billion a year. It's sold in more than 122 countries. The company has more than 15,000 workers. Fielding and Chavannes would be amazed. They were just trying to make wallpaper. But they turned failure into success.

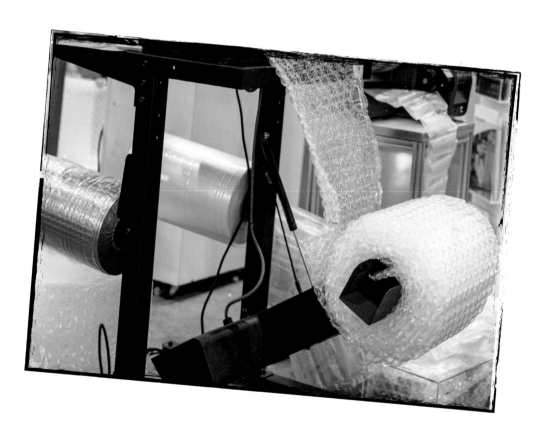

SUCCESS STORY!
The First Phone

Alexander Graham Bell was an inventor. He is credited with inventing the telephone. His invention was a success. It changed our lives. Phones have been used for more than 150 years. They're used in homes. They're used in businesses. The story about the first phone call is famous. It happened on March 10, 1876. Bell called Thomas Watson. Watson was his assistant. He was in the next room. Bell said, "Mr. Watson, come here. I want to see you." Bell died on August 2, 1922. Telephone service in the United States and Canada stopped for one minute the day he was buried. This was done to honor him.

LEARN MORE

Books

Bader, Bonnie. *Who was Alexander Graham Bell?* New York: Penguin Workshop, 2013.

Jones, Charlotte Foltz. *Mistakes That Worked: The World's Familiar Inventions and How They Came to Be.* New York: Delacorte Press, 2016.

Tech Tron. *The Most Famous Inventors Who Ever Lived: Inventors Guide for Kids.* Tech Tron, 2017.

Websites

With an adult, explore more online with these suggested searches.

"Inventions," Kids Discover

"Inventions," Time for Kids

"Invention Process," Inventive Kids

GLOSSARY

acrylic (uh-KRIH-lik) quick-drying synthetic fiber

adhesive (ad-HEE-siv) a substance that makes things stick, such as glue or cement

beakers (BEE-kerz) deep cups or glasses often used for scientific experiments

dye (DYE) liquid used for coloring clothes or other products

flop (FLAHP) to fail

fragile (FRA-juhl) easily broken or damaged

greenhouse (GREEN-hows) a structure used to grow plants year-round

insulation (in-suh-LAY-shuhn) filling used in between building walls to help keep heat in or out

malaria (muh-LAIR-ee-uh) a sickness caused by a parasite that invades red blood cells

mauve (MAWV) a pale purple color

patented (PA-tuhnt-id) registered with the government and holding sole right to make and sell an invention

perfume (PER-fyoom) a pleasant-smelling liquid

persistence (per-SIH-stuhns) the will to keep trying after first failing or experiencing challenges

quinine (KWYE-nyn) a substance made from cinchona bark and used in medicine

synthetic (sin-THEH-tik) something produced with chemicals instead of natural ingredients

INDEX

ABOUT THE AUTHOR

Martin Gitlin is an educational book author based in Connecticut. He won more than 45 awards as a newspaper sportswriter from 1991 to 2002. Included was a first-place award from the Associated Press for his coverage of the 1995 World Series. He has had more than 200 books published since 2006. Most of them were written for students.

Failure is part
of life, and the old adage
"try, try again" is at the center of
this high-interest series. Explore the
fascinating and fantastic failures that
became some of the world's greatest
successes. There's no limit to
what ingenuity and resilience
can do to turn a flop
into a fortune.

BOOKS IN THIS SERIES INCLUDE

Business Innovations Made by Mistake • Delicious Food Mishaps
Surprising Starts of Health and Hygiene Products
Failures Turned into Tech Fortunes • Favorite Toys Made from Failures
Failures That Fueled Transportation

45TH PARALLEL PRESS TITLES FEATURE:

High-interest topics with accessible reading levels
Considerate vocabulary
Engaging content and fascinating facts
Clear text and formatting
Compelling photos

ISBN-13: 978-1668939260

9 781668 939260

45°

45TH PARALLEL PRESS